BLUES ALL BLUES

Contents

Feeling the Blues - Level 1	4
Feeling the Blues - Level 2	6
Feeling the Blues - Level 3	8
Feeling the Blues - Stride	10
Back Alley Blues - Level 1	12
Back Alley Blues - Level 2	14
Back Alley Blues - Level 3	16
Back Alley Blues - Stride	18
Marching Blues - Level 2	20
Marching Blues - Level 3	22
Marching Blues - Level 4	24
Sidewalk Blues - Level 2	26
Clarinet Blues - Level 2	28
Cornerbar Blues - Level 2	30
Big Band Blues - Level 3	32
Jammin' Da Blues - Level 4	34

Joe de Navas

Visit us at: amazon.com / books blues de Navas

PROGRESSIVE LEARNING

With a stable left hand rhythm, the right hand weaves a melody filling it with colorful harmonies.

To help you achieve this goal, I have organized the examples in this book in progressive levels, so that you will improve your skills and knowledge of the blues techniques gradually, one step at a time:

Level one :   The melodies are presented in a very basic arrangement so you get acquainted with it and your fingers can easily play it.

Level two: Same melody as level one, with some chords on the right hand interpretation and more rhythm notes on the left hand.

Level three: Same melody as in the preceeding levels with a more advanced arrangement, filled with colorful harmonies for you to discover.

Stride: This is another way to perform these blues melodies. It will help you get a good swing and also you can mix it with the other left hand motions in your interpretations:

Level four: Again a more advanced arrangement of the melodie that requires higher skills.

Study the exercises in an orderly way, learning them by heart one at a time.. Do not jump to the next exercise until you have memorized correctly the one before. When playing, use a "free swing" with which you can comfortably follow your own pace.

FEELING THE BLUES - level 1

FEELING THE BLUES - level 2

FEELING THE BLUES - level 3

FEELING THE BLUES - Stride

BACK ALLEY BLUES - level 1

12

BACK ALLEY BLUES - level 2

14

BACK ALLEY BLUES - level 3

17

BACK ALLEY BLUES - Stride

MARCHING BLUES - level 2

MARCHING BLUES - level 3

23

MARCHING BLUES - level 4

SIDEWALK BLUES - level 2

26

CLARINET BLUES - level 2

28

CORNERBAR BLUES - level 3

30

BIG BAND BLUES - level 4

En este ejemplo introduzco el GLISSANDO, es decir: con la uña del dedo gordo de la mano derecha dirigida hacia abajo y empezando aproximadamente en el sexto SOL del teclado, deslice la mano en sentido descendente para producir un efecto cascada.

JAMMIN' DA BLUES - level 4

39

Printed in Great Britain
by Amazon